ERIC PORTERFIELD

Law School Essay Exams

Mastering Issue Spotting Essay Hypotheticals

First edition

This book was professionally typeset on Reedsy.
Find out more at reedsy.com

Contents

1

Chapter One: Introduction

Who should read this book? This book is primarily designed for law students who have just started, or are just about to start, law school. The best time to read this book is *before* your first law school assessment, such as a quiz, midterm, or final exam. The terminology and strategies in this book will make the most sense to those who have already started their first year or "1L" year of law school. If you are committed to attending law school, however, this book will still be of benefit to you. I recommend that you read it now and then revisit it once you have begun your first year of law school. This book will also benefit you even if you have already taken assessments in some of your classes. It is never too late to improve your performance on law school essay exams – the principal way law students are assessed in the vast majority of classes.

Why listen to me? Simply put, using the method I describe in this book, I excelled in law school. I not only made As in all of my first-year classes, I made the highest grade in the class in 13 of the 15 classes I took and the second highest grade in the class in the remaining two. I graduated as the class valedictorian and finished with not only a GPA higher than the rest of my class, but one of the highest GPAs ever recorded for any class in the history of my law school. I went on to clerk for a federal judge, work at a highly respected law firm, get a graduate law degree from Harvard Law School, and become a law professor, where I teach my students the same strategies I lay out here.

What are my goals for you? After reading this book, I want you to be able to take the rules you learn in your class reading assignments and class discussions and turn them into a manageable and digestible outline, which you can memorize and use to master your law school essay exams – the type of assessment you are most likely to encounter during law school, especially in your typical "1L" classes such as contracts, torts, civil procedure, and more.

Let's start with some terminology and background. I have mentioned the term "assessment" and noted it includes quizzes, midterms, and final exams. Historically, law school has taught the same subjects and assessed students the same way – one end-of-term final exam, all essay in format. Law schools are only recently moving to using multiple assessments of different formats, but the dominant method of assessing law student performance, particularly in the crucial first year courses, remains the all-essay final exam. Don't worry if your professor also uses multiple choice questions. The process you will follow as described in his book to outline and learn the rules will also help you choose the best answer in multiple choice questions. Law school essay exams consist of a hypothetical or series of hypotheticals in which events transpire, e.g., people say and do things, promises are made and broken, transactions take place, people are harmed physically and/or financially, possible wrongs occur, and people sue and are sued. Your job as a law student is to take the rules you have learned and apply them to the facts – the events, transactions, and occurrences in the essay hypothetical – and resolve the issues presented in the hypothetical.

Why do we use the term hypothetical? It is merely a synonym for fact pattern; essentially a hypothetical is a fictitious story. It is a series of hypothetical facts, called a hypothetical because it is not real or actual. It is hypothetical in the sense that it is differentiated from the facts and events you read about in cases – those facts actually happened and courts actually resolved the issues or conflicts presented by those facts.

What is an issue? An issue is a conflict or potential conflict that legal rules are designed to resolve. Consider this hypothetical: You are driving your car on a public street in State A and, while texting and driving, you collide with a pedestrian walking in a crosswalk, breaking her legs and causing her to be hospitalized. This is a very short, single-sentence hypothetical. What is the issue that it presents? One benefit you have as a first-year student is that you need not wonder what set of rules you need to bring to bear to resolve any issues you find. If you are given this sentence as part of a torts exam, an obvious issue would be whether you, the driver, are liable to the pedestrian under the rules of tort law for her personal injuries. Using the law you have learned in torts, you might posit that the law of negligence applies and helps resolve whether the driver is liable to the pedestrian. If, however, you are given this question in a civil procedure exam, the issue is more likely to be whether a lawsuit in State A is permissible or advisable. More on the rules is to come.

What sort of courses are likely to use this assessment model? This model of essay hypotheticals is fair game for any law school class. This model remains prevalent in first-year law school courses. What courses are those? They vary from law school to law school. The variance, however, is not dramatic. Many if not most law schools dictate that entering law students take courses in the following subjects during their first year of law school: contracts, torts, civil procedure, property, criminal law, criminal procedure, legal research and writing, and constitutional law.[1] Legal research is a class that focuses on the skill

---

1 https://lawpreview.barbri.com/law-school-curriculum/

of researching the law and writing like a lawyer and is usually assessed with written work that does not fall into the essay exam hypothetical I have described above. The remaining classes do. Your professor may define them differently, but just so we can be on the same page for purpose of this book, I will give you my basic definition of three classes I will refer to in this book: contracts, torts, and civil procedure. Contracts is the study of how enforceable agreements are formed, what is considered a breach of a contract or agreement, and the damages for such breaches. Torts is the study of civil wrongs – essentially when acts or omissions that cause harm can give rise to civil liability, usually in the form of money damages. Civil Procedure is the study of how parties bring civil (as opposed to criminal) lawsuits and the rules they must abide by in advancing and defending against claims in court.

2

Chapter Two: The Rules

Where do I get the rules I will use to solve legal issues on the exam? This is where your reading assignments and class discussions come in. In most cases, the rules will not be served up on a silver platter. You must work to determine what the rules are that you are supposed to memorize. You likely will not be given the rules the same way you might be given the equations you use to solve problems in math or scientific endeavors. You must learn to read legal sources and distill the rules from those sources. Often, the rules you formulate will come from multiple sources. You will likely read some combination of cases, statutes, textbooks, hornbooks, treatises, and restatements in order to compile the rules that you will need to memorize now so you can use them on your essay exams and that you will need to retain for later use on the bar exam. A comprehensive description of legal sources and the differences between them (e.g., primary versus secondary and binding versus persuasive) is beyond the scope of this book. So too is a comprehensive teaching of how to extract and synthesize legal rules from multiple sources. Instead, this chapter will posit a few rules across each of three first-year courses: contracts, torts, and civil procedure.

Let's begin with contracts. One of the natural first rules to learn is the rule that governs which set of rules you must apply depending on the nature of the alleged contract in the hypothetical. You may have heard the term common law by now. This is essentially the body of judge-made law that has been handed down over time rather than laws that are created by legislatures. The common law is how much of the law of contracts, torts, property, and criminal law has evolved over time. Today, states have adopted the UCC or Uniform Commercial Code, which replaces or supplants the common law with respect to certain types of contracts. The UCC applies to contracts that involve the sale of goods. What is a good? The UCC defines a good as any tangible thing moveable at the time of identification to the contract. If the contract does not principally deal with the sale of goods – for example, the contract is for the sale of real estate or is a contract to provide services (neither of which are "moveable things") – then the common law rules apply. So we now have our first rule in contracts that will go in our outline:

"The Uniform Commercial Code applies to contracts for the sale of goods, which are tangible things moveable at the time of identification to the contract."

What is an outline? And if you feel like I felt at the beginning of law school, you are asking "why is it everyone else seems to know what it is and I don't?" Stay tuned for the next chapter. For now, we need some more rules before we can jump into outlining those rules.

Another common rule to learn early on in contracts is what the elements are of an enforceable contract. A contract requires an offer to be communicated and accepted, and the contract must be supported by consideration. We now have another rule for our outline:

"An enforceable contract requires (1) an offer, (2) that is accepted, and (3) that is supported by consideration."

What is an offer? Under the common law, an offer must be promissory in character, (often using terms such as "I promise" or "I will" or "I shall"), create a reasonable belief in the offeree that acceptance will conclude the bargain, and state a price for the promise. Here is a third rule for our outline:

"An offer must be: (1) promissory in character, (2) create a reasonable belief in the offeree that acceptance will conclude the bargain, and (3) state a price for the promise."

Now let's consider another first-year course, torts. Many first-year torts courses will cover intentional torts such as battery as well as the tort of negligence. In my experience, many torts courses begin with intentional torts. From your reading assignments, which likely include reading key tort cases and perhaps a hornbook or treatise written by an expert on tort law, you could come up with the following rule for the intentional tort of battery:

"A battery occurs when: (1) the actor acts intentionally, (2) touching the victim's person, and (3) the touching is harmful or offensive to a reasonable person."

As with contracts above when we considered that a contract requires an offer and we drilled down into what constitutes an offer, you do the same with torts. Your introductory torts course will also spend significant time and effort to explain some of these key terms found in the rule you have formulated for battery: What does it mean to act intentionally? What counts as touching the victim's person? And what is harmful or offensive to a reasonable person? It is often said that for conduct to qualify as intentional in torts does not mean that the actor intended the result of her actions. Rather, the actor need only have engaged in intentional conduct. The motive is not dispositive. Even if the actor only meant the contact as a joke or was "just kidding," if the actor behaved in a way that made the touching substantially certain, the why does not matter. The actor has acted intentionally. That brings us to another rule for our outline:

"An actor need not intend the consequences of her action to act intentionally. Even if the actor's motive was only to joke or kid, an act is intentional where the actor engages in conduct substantially certain to cause contact."

Similarly, you will learn more about what it means to touch the victim's person. Does that literally mean that only contact with the victim's body counts? No. The law of torts tells us that touching includes the actual person of the victim as well as anything intimately associated with the victim. This includes things connected to the victim like clothing, a backpack slung over the shoulders, or an umbrella in the victim's hand. Indirect contact also qualifies. Now we have another rule:

"A touching for the purposes of battery includes contact with the victim's person and/or anything intimately associated with the victim such as items worn or carried."

Let's conclude the rules section with a different kind of first-year course, civil procedure. Civil procedure differs from contracts and torts because civil procedure does not concern what rights and obligations people owe one another in daily life. Rather, civil procedure governs people's conduct in litigation, including in court. Civil procedure is also different in that courses like torts and contracts are teaching you the rules that likely exist in the several states, as the law of what is an enforceable contract and the law of what is an actionable tort is essentially state law. Because civil procedure is a little different, the rules also look a little different. First, the rules will concern things like where and how a case may be brought. Secondly, the course is technically "Federal Civil Procedure," which, as the name communicates, concentrates on federal law, not state law. One of the first doctrines you are likely to encounter in federal civil procedure is the doctrine of subject matter jurisdiction. Subject matter jurisdiction is the authority of the court (jurisdiction) to hear and resolve a certain type of case (subject matter). Federal courts are courts of limited jurisdiction. They cannot simply hear and resolve any case brought to them. Rather, they can only hear certain types of cases. One of those types of cases involve cases between citizens of different states where the amount in controversy is more than $75,000.00. These are called "diversity" cases. So we have our first civil procedure rule for our outline:

"A federal court may hear cases between citizens of different states where the amount in controversy exceeds the sum or value of $75,000.00, exclusive of costs and interest."

As above, many of these terms in our rule need further definitions – i.e., their own rules. What does it mean to be a citizen of a state? We normally think of citizenship in terms of allegiance to a nation. But for purposes of federal civil procedure, we have to determine what makes someone a citizen of a state. Unlike U.S. citizenship, a citizen is not a citizen of a state just because she was born there. Rather, an individual – a natural person (provided she is also a U.S. citizen) – is a citizen of the state of her domicile. Of course, that begs the question: what is a person's domicile? A person is domiciled in the state in which she physically resides with the intent to remain indefinitely. It is also true that a person can change her domicile and thus her citizenship. She does not lose her old domicile unless and until she actually moves and physically resides in a new state while also having the intent to remain in that new state indefinitely. And what does indefinite mean? It means you do not have any *definite* plan to leave; you intend your stay to be of an indeterminate length. This is our second rule:

"A natural person who is a U.S. citizen is a citizen of the state in which she is domiciled, meaning the state in which she physically resides with the intent to remain indefinitely. A person's intent to remain indefinitely means the person has no fixed plan to leave. A person can change her domicile by taking up residence in a new state with the intent to remain indefinitely. A person can have only one domicile at a time and does not lose her old domicile until a new one is established."

That gives us a few rules across three different first-year classes. Now we turn to outlining.

3

Chapter Three: Outlining

What is outlining? And as I said before, if you are anything like I was in law school, you are wondering not only what outlining is, but also why everyone else seems to know what it is and have it down. An outline is basically a tool. Maybe a better way is to describe the outline is as a tool*box*. Your outline should contain all the rules you will need to resolve the legal issues that come up in your essay exam. So that seems pretty simple: learn the rules from your readings and class discussions, record those rules in your outline, study your outline for the exam, and write out excellent answers to your essay exam questions.

The problem for me was that my outline did not seem like a very useful tool. Or if I thought of it is a toolbox, it seemed to be overflowing. I wrote down salient facts from cases, things I thought of as rules, and much more, not wanting to miss anything. My outline was typed into a Word document in outline form – i.e., Roman Numeral I in Torts would say "Intentional Torts" and Capital A underneath would say "Battery." It proceeded in linear form. Under Battery would be lines and lines and even pages and pages of details from cases, in-class hypotheticals, and explanations about what various theories of why we have the tort of battery, as well as the elements of battery – although this last part was often fairly hard to pick out. My outline was thorough. It was also dense. And it seemed too long as a viable study aid. Regardless of the class, it seemed to grow to fifty pages in length. But it seemed like everyone else was outlining that way. All the smart students seemed to have the same dense, word-packed, linear outline. I even went to talk to my Legal Writing professor, who seemed the most approachable and least like Professor Kingsfield from the Paper Chase. (If you haven't already seen it, don't bother; you don't need any more anxiety about the first year of law school at this point.) He showed me his outlines from law school and all that did is drive my anxiety through the roof. His outlines were not only dense, linear, and jam packed with information, they were long. So long they filled up a two-inch three-ring binder.

This is the point at which I had sort of a crisis about whether I could be successful at law school. Professors were telling us that this is not undergrad anymore folks – memorization is not going to cut it. Maybe in college you could just memorize things your professor said or emphasized in the readings and regurgitate them on the exam. But professors were calling us to do more than memorize – you have to be able to use the rules. You have to be able to do a higher order mental exercise: you must apply the rules to novel factual situations and predict outcomes based on how those rules work. How can I apply the rules if I do not know them? And I don't need to simply have passing familiarity with the rules, I have to know them. Cold. Law school classes had sharpened for me the idea that words matter. And the slightest difference in terms – leaving a word out, substituting a synonym for another word, adding words that don't belong – can drastically change the outcome. What I needed was a simple method that would help me dedicate the rules to memory in a way that I could quickly recite them for the exam and use my limited time to think on analysis or applying the rules to the essay exam hypothetical. The tool I decided on was index or note cards. I used 3" by 5" cards or 4" by 6" cards. It is a matter of personal preference and mostly depends on the size of your handwriting. I advise you to handwrite at least the first draft even if you want to type out your rule statements on your index cards. You can go buy cards or print them from your word processing program yourself using templates that are easy to find online.

Let's begin with contracts again. Some rules were easy to put on a note card. Recall our first rule example from contracts above.

The UCC rather than the common law of contract applies to:

1. contracts for the sale of goods, which are

    a. all tangible things
    b. that are moveable
    c. at the time of identification to the contact.

This rule easily fit on *one side* of a three by five card. One side is important for at least a couple of reasons. First, the whole point of using index or note cards is to make memorizing the content easier. The index card is intended to be digestible and in stark contrast to the typically dense, detail-packed linear outline. Second, to use the index card as a study tool, the other side is reserved for a prompt – a question that will trigger you to recite the rule stated on the reverse of the index card. For example:

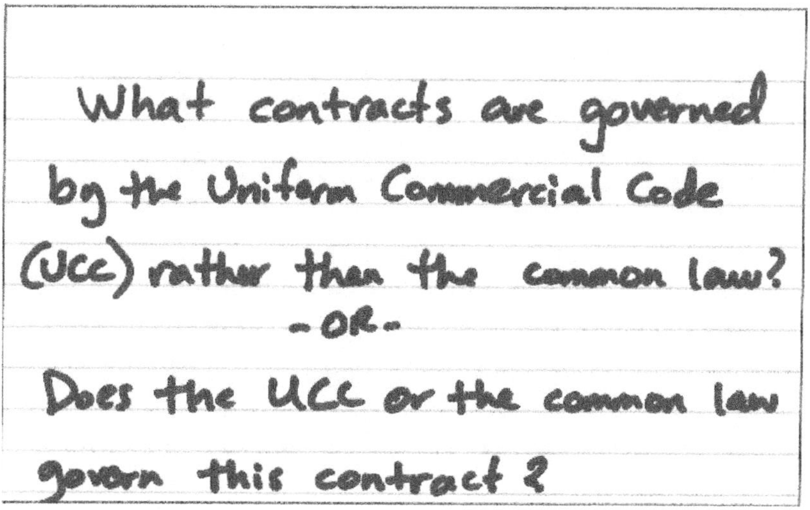
What contracts are governed by the Uniform Commercial Code (UCC) rather than the common law?
-OR-
Does the UCC or the common law govern this contract?

Notice that you can state that prompt in more than one way. I have stated it two different ways; the first is a question you might ask yourself, the other sounds more like an issue statement you might write. We will talk more about issue statements when we address in more detail the format of responding to essay exam hypotheticals – namely, IRAC (Issue, Rule, Analysis/Application, and Conclusion) or CRAC (Conclusion, Rule, Analysis/Application, Conclusion).

Other rule statements were harder to fit on an index card. At first, I tried to put every applicable rule I could think of for common law contract formation on one card. The prompt or issue statement side easily fit on one side:

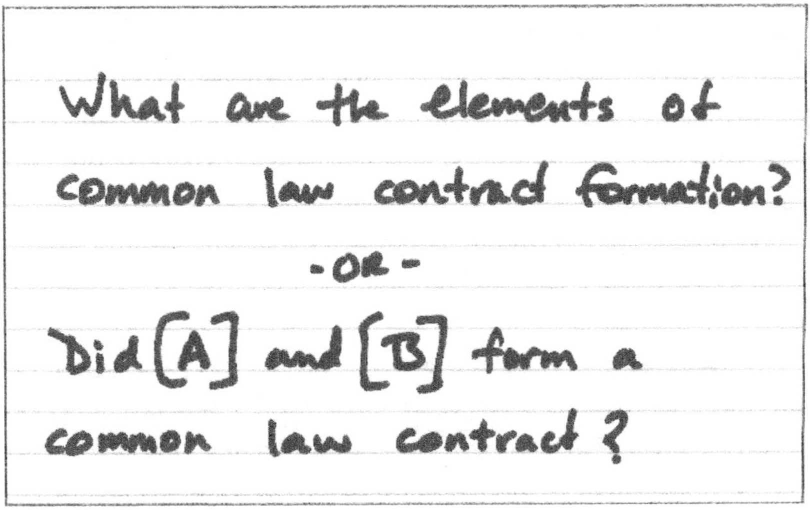
What are the elements of common law contract formation?

-OR-

Did [A] and [B] form a common law contract?

The rule side of my index card for the elements of contact formation, however, started off looking like this cluttered image:

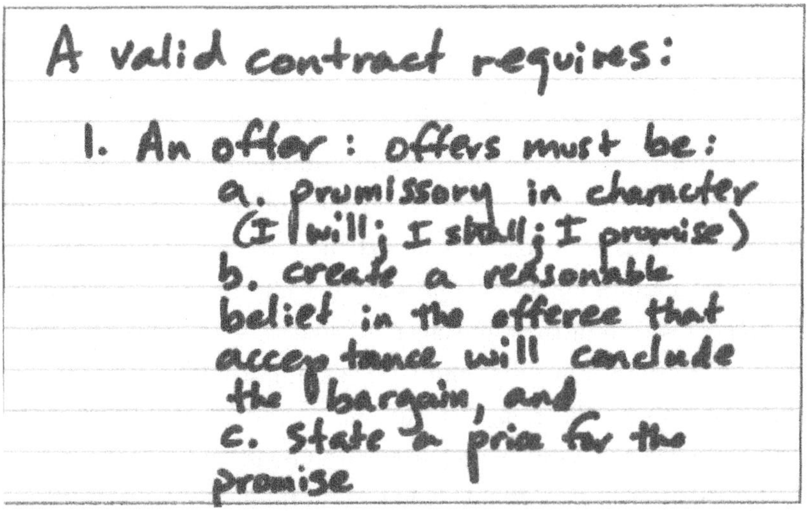
A valid contract requires:

1. An offer: offers must be:
   a. promissory in character (I will; I shall; I promise)
   b. create a reasonable belief in the offeree that acceptance will conclude the bargain, and
   c. state a price for the promise

But where are acceptance and consideration? I ran out of room. It quickly became apparent that using an index card that tried to give the elements of a contract, i.e. offer, acceptance, and consideration, and also tried to define or state the rules (sometimes called "sub-rules") for what is an offer, what is an acceptance, and what is consideration was barely any better than the dense, unusable, linear outline it was meant to replace. As a result, I decided each of these rules or sub-rules needed its own index card. Thus, the basic elements of a contract ended up looking like this:

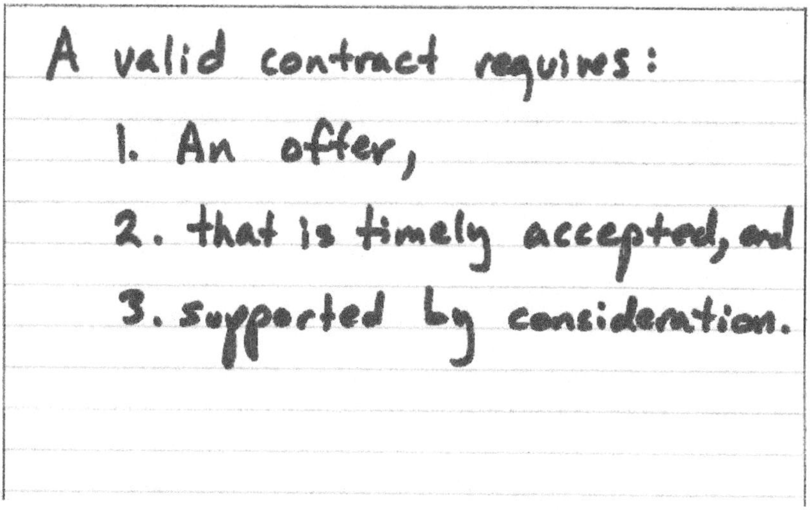
A valid contract requires:
1. An offer,
2. that is timely accepted, and
3. supported by consideration.

And the rule for an offer ended up looking like this:

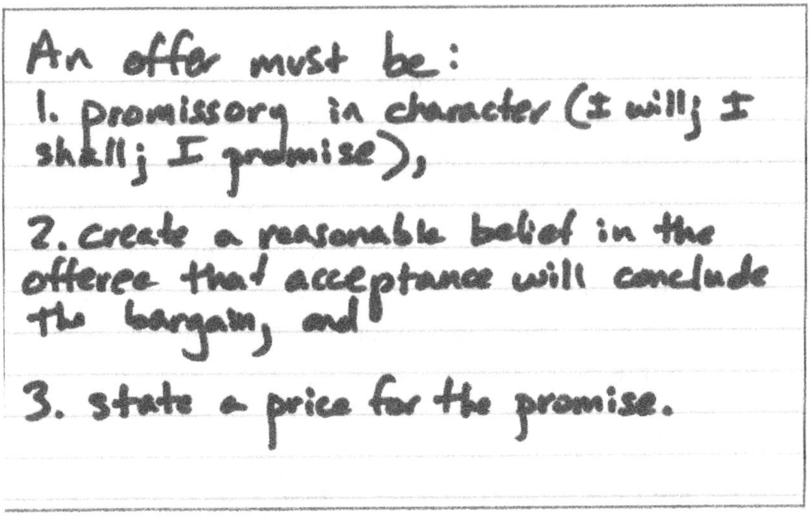
An offer must be:
1. promissory in character (I will; I shall; I promise),
2. create a reasonable belief in the offeree that acceptance will conclude the bargain, and
3. state a price for the promise.

The reverse side of the offer index card with the prompt or issue statement looked like this:

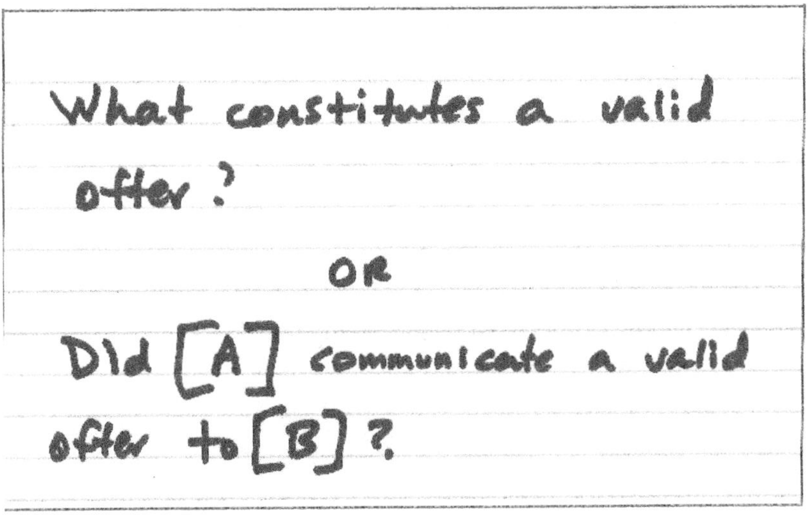
What constitutes a valid offer?

OR

Did [A] communicate a valid offer to [B]?

When it came time to write out the rule for an acceptance, it suffered from the same density problem as trying to state the elements of a contract and all of the definitions of those elements on a single index card. It looked like this:

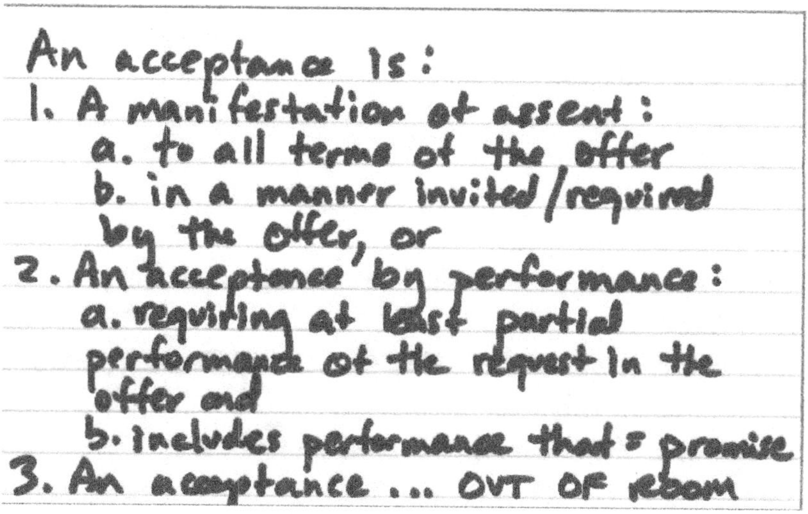
An acceptance is:
1. A manifestation of assent:
   a. to all terms of the offer
   b. in a manner invited/required by the offer, or
2. An acceptance by performance:
   a. requiring at least partial performance of the request in the offer and
   b. includes performance that = promise
3. An acceptance ... OUT OF ROOM

Instead, acceptance became its own rule with its own index card and the various types of acceptances became their own rules with their own index cards:

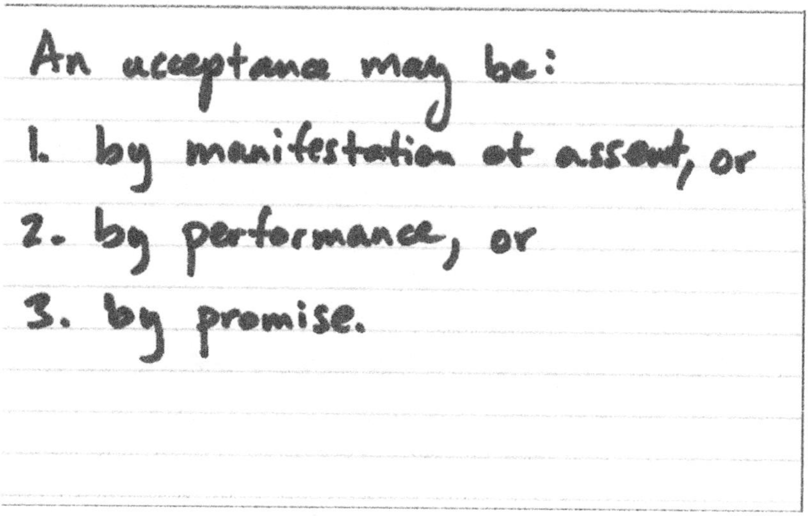
An acceptance may be:
1. by manifestation of assent, or
2. by performance, or
3. by promise.

Now let's turn to torts. The rule for battery fits well on an index card, provided we don't try to squeeze the rules for what intent means, what touching means, and what harmful or offensive and the reasonable person standard mean:

> A battery occurs when:
> 1. An actor acts intentionally,
> 2. touching the victim's person, and
> 3. the touching is harmful or offensive to a reasonable person.

The reverse or prompt/issue statement side of the card looks like this:

> What constitutes a battery?
>
> -OR-
>
> Is [A's] conduct toward [B] a battery?

The rule statement for intent has its own index card:

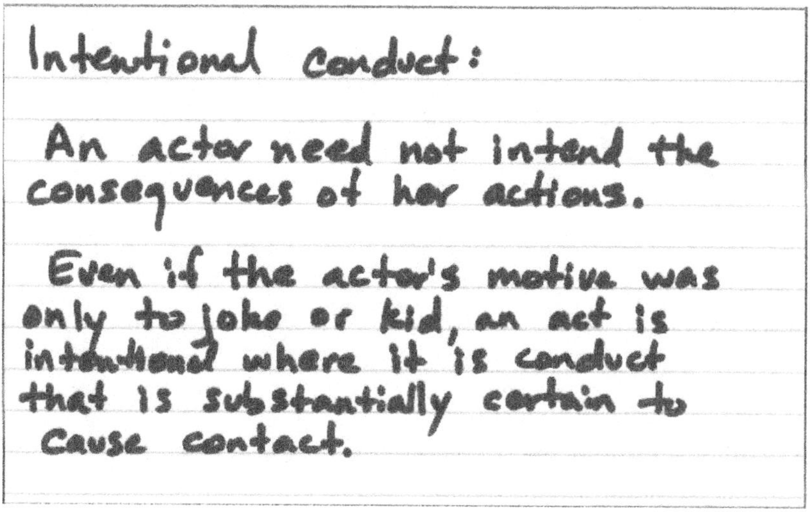
Intentional conduct:

An actor need not intend the consequences of her actions.

Even if the actor's motive was only to joke or kid, an act is intentional where it is conduct that is substantially certain to cause contact.

The prompt/issue statement side of the intent card looks like this:

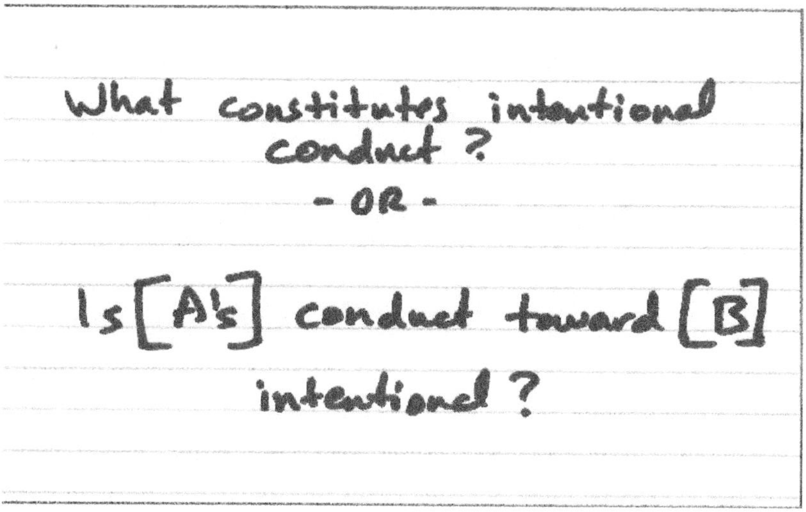
What constitutes intentional conduct?

- OR -

Is [A's] conduct toward [B] intentional?

Similarly, the rule for a touching has its own index card:

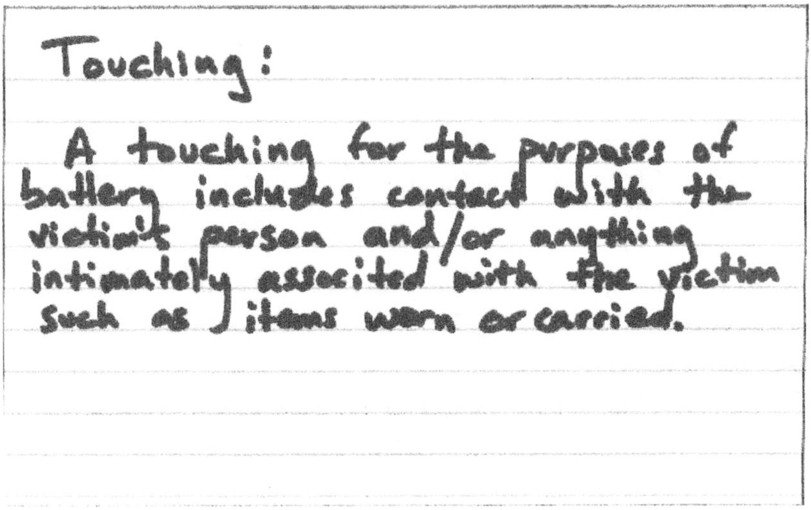

The other side of the index card for touching looks like this:

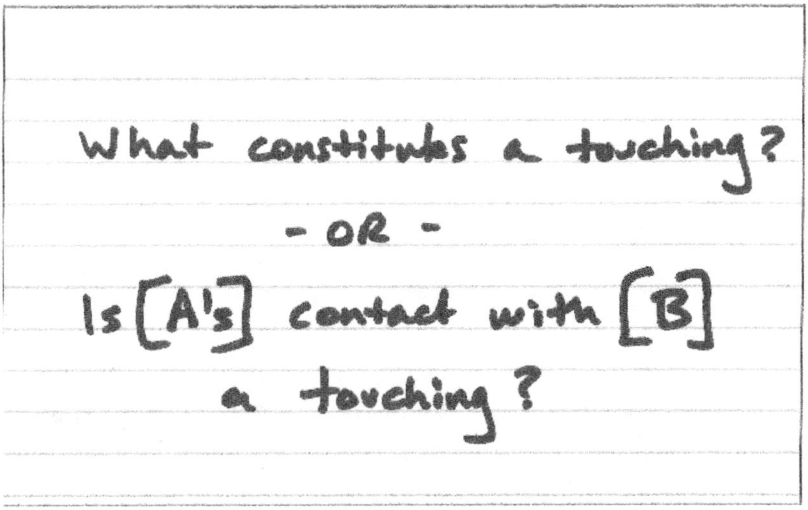

Let's finish with civil procedure. Having learned from contracts above, the basic rule of diversity of citizenship subject matter jurisdiction gets its own index card and other rules (or sub-rules) about matters such as citizenship get their own index card. Here is the index card for the basic rule of diversity of citizenship subject matter jurisdiction:

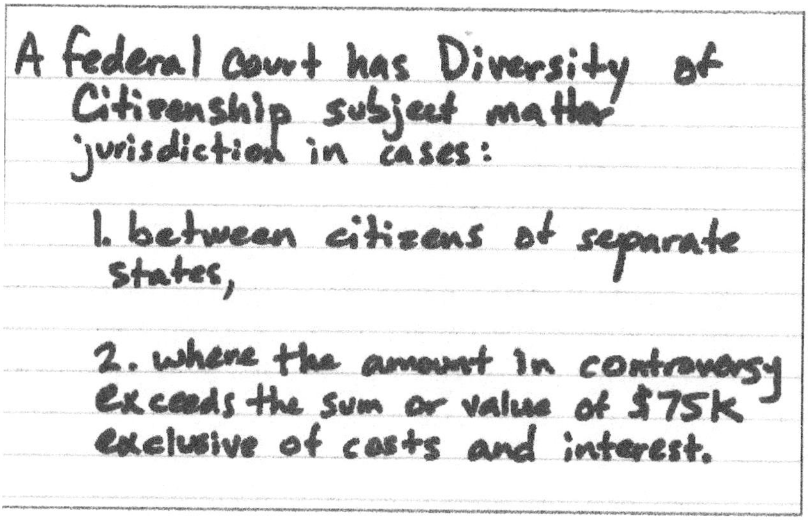
A federal court has Diversity of Citizenship subject matter jurisdiction in cases:

1. between citizens of separate states,

2. where the amount in controversy exceeds the sum or value of $75k exclusive of costs and interest.

The prompt/issue statement side of the diversity card looks like this:

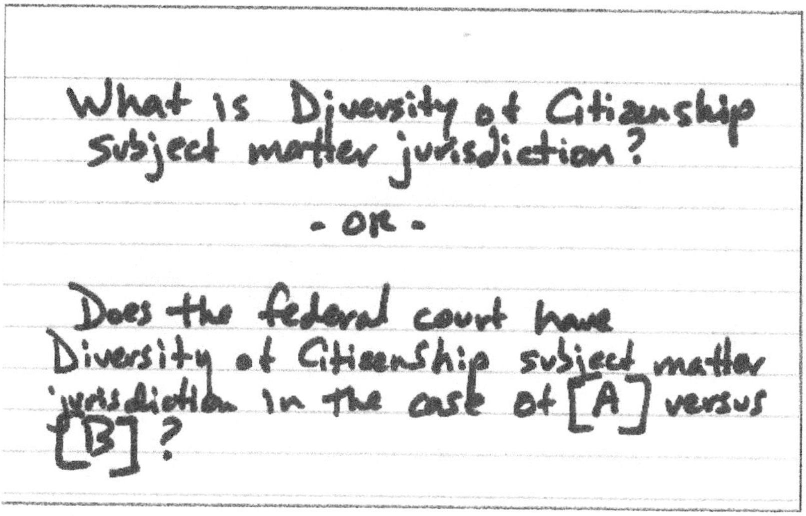
What is Diversity of Citizenship subject matter jurisdiction?

- OR -

Does the federal court have Diversity of Citizenship subject matter jurisdiction in the case of [A] versus [B]?

What it means to be a citizen of a state for diversity purposes will not fit neatly on this card so it gets its own index card:

Citizenship - Natural Persons

A natural person who is a U.S. citizen is a citizen of the state in which she is domiciled.

Domicile is the place one physically resides with the intent to remain indefinitely. Indefinite intent means no fixed plan to leave.

The prompt/issue statement for the citizenship card looks like this:

How is state citizenship of natural persons who are U.S. citizens determined?

- OR -

Of what state is [A], a natural person and U.S. citizen, a citizen?

As you will learn, there is much more to say about citizenship. As with the contracts section above, not every rule concerning citizenship will fit on one index card. For example, there is a rule about how to change one's citizenship. And as you can infer from the wording of the citizenship rule, there is a separate rule for natural persons who are aliens – people who are not U.S. citizens – as well as for parties who are not natural persons – in fact there are multiple rules. The rule about changing citizenship for natural persons who are U.S. citizens looks like this:

> **Change of Citizenship - Natural Persons**
>
> A person who is a U.S. citizen can change her domicile and thus her state citizenship by taking up residence in a new state with the intent to remain indefinitely.
>
> A person has only one domicile at a time and does not lose her old domicile until a new one is established.

The prompt/issue statement side of the change of citizenship index card looks like this:

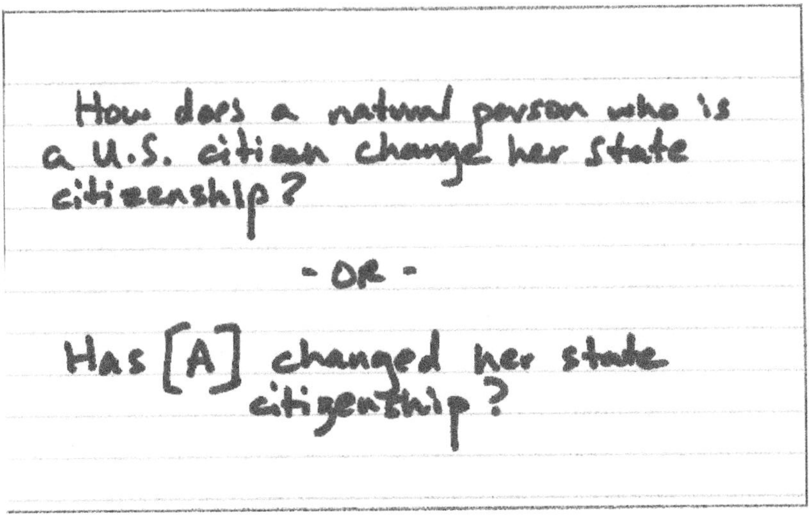

Now that you have some index cards created, how do you use them? As an initial matter, just creating and revising and re-creating the note cards will go a long way to helping you memorize the rules. But once you feel you have the cards in a usable form, you begin the process of committing them all to memory. Pick a subject. Let's start with contracts. Take all of your index cards and stack them face down. That means the rule statement should be on the back and the visible side – the side facing you – should contain the prompt or issue statement you have decided on. Pick up the first card and ask yourself, out loud, "what are the elements of common law contract formation?" Then say, again out loud, "the elements of a valid contract are an offer, an acceptance, and consideration." Then turn the card over. Compare your voiced answer to the writing on your card. Did you get it exactly right? Great! Put that card in a discard pile. Did you just get close? Or maybe not even close? Put the card on the bottom of the deck of cards in your hand so you will encounter it again. Go through the deck again and again, putting cards you get exactly right in the discard pile and the others back at the bottom of the deck. Set a schedule to do this. Every night for a set period of time, every weekend until you make it once through the deck, 10 cards a day – you know better than anyone when you have study time. But that doesn't mean you restrict yourself to looking at your index cards only at certain times. You can also switch it up a bit. Have a study partner? Have her hold the cards. She will ask you out loud: "what are the elements of common law contract formation?" And you will respond out loud. This will not only imprint the rules on your memory, it will help the study partner asking the questions. Another great thing about a stack of index cards with a big rubber band around it is you are not lugging around a computer, you don't need an electrical outlet, and internet connectivity is not an issue. Do you have a doctor's appointment? Bet you're going to spend more than a few minutes in a waiting room. Take your contracts cards with you and see how many you can get through before your name is called. Getting an oil change? Take some torts cards with you and drill yourself on intentional torts. Index cards are especially conducive to studying when and where you have time.

Why do you need to say "what are the elements of common law contract formation?" and "a common law contract requires an offer, an acceptance, and consideration" out loud? When you look at the words on the index card, you are storing those words and images in your memory using a visual pathway. When you say the words aloud, you are reinforcing this memory by also using an auditory pathway. And handling physical cards stimulates you to learn kinesthetically as well. Maybe you already know your learning style or styles and which ones are optimal for you. Maybe you do not. Even if you do, why not maximize the ways your brain can learn the material?

Why do you need a discard pile? As you have probably already learned, there are three elements to a contract: offer, acceptance, and consideration. How much more time do you need to study that? Put it in the discard pile. Now you have one less card to focus on. You also have more time to commit to memory the more difficult rules. As you get to the end of the semester and final exams, you will likely find that the intimidating stack of index cards you had just a few weeks ago has dwindled to maybe a dozen or so cards. These cards will be the most complicated or convoluted rules and you will be able to devote much more time to those rules. You will not have to guess which rules you know and do not know – you will not have to rely on some emotional reaction to a rule. You will know you know the rules in the discard pile the way you need to know them – cold. How will you know? Because they don't make it in the discard pile unless you master them. And you will know which rules need more attention. They are still in your stack. Waiting for you to recite them perfectly.

4

Chapter Four: Using the Rules on Your Essay Exam

Why is it you need to memorize these rules? Recall what you are doing with these cards. Memorization is the absolute minimum. It is the ante in to the game. Without it, you are not even playing, let alone capable of winning. You should be using these cards to facilitate memorization. But you must also be able to apply these rules. If you are only memorizing these rules the way you might memorize a famous speech, a Shakespearean soliloquy, or a poem in a foreign language, you will be missing a crucial part. When I would look at my contracts cards, I would say a contract requires an offer, an acceptance, and consideration. Then when I pulled out "offer," I would say "an offer must be promissory in character, create a reasonable belief in the offeree that acceptance will conclude the bargain, and state a price for the promise." Then as I sat there feeling good about having nailed the rule, I would ask myself, how is this going to come up? What does "promissory language" mean? I did not make a card that further defined what counted as promissory language. But you could if you wanted. I would say to myself – I remember a case where someone said "I will" and "will" counted. But there was some case where someone said something like "I sure would like to get $10 for this book" and the court said something like that is not the same as a promise – "would like" is not the same as "will." How about the second element like "reasonable belief that acceptance will conclude the bargain"? Again, you could have another card for this concept. Or you can rely on examples in your brain and your ability to argue whether it is or is not reasonable for someone to conclude that a bargain is imminent. Using language like "I would" would make one think there are more steps to be taken. So using language like "would" probably fails at the second step as well. The key here is to think like your professor. How will she test me on this rule? Come up with your own hypotheticals. The cases you read will help you do this. For example, here is a really brief hypothetical that implicates the rules we have on our index cards for contracts:

A and B are neighbors. One day, as A and B were both checking their mailboxes, A shouted to B: "hey, I love your house." B replied "I wish someone would take it off my hands." A responded "I actually could probably come up with the money." B said "great. It is all yours buddy. I hope you enjoy it." Then both A and B laughed and walked back in their houses. Later that day, A knocked on B's door and B answered. A said "I found a bank that will finance it for me! When can I get the keys?" B said "Whoa, friend. It isn't for sale." A responded "But we had a deal!"

The essay question may give you a specific prompt. Do A and B have a contract? Or it might simply say identify all issues, the rules that govern the resolution of those issues, apply the rules to the facts, and come to a conclusion.

Your answer to the latter sort of prompt might look something like this:

The first issue is what law will govern whether there is a contract formed between A and B. Is this alleged contract governed by the Uniform Commercial Code or the common law of contracts?

The Uniform Commercial Code (UCC) rather than the common law of contracts governs contracts for the sale of goods, which are all tangible things moveable at the time of identification to the contract.

Here, the common law of contracts will apply and govern. The subject of the contract is B's home, which is real property, not a good. Although real property is a tangible thing and the purported contract seems to concern a sale (as opposed to a lease), B's real property is not movable. Because movability of the thing is an essential requirement for qualifying as a good, the UCC will not govern.

Accordingly, because the purported contract deals with non-movable real property rather than a sale of a movable good, the common law of contracts rather than the UCC will govern this transaction.

Your next issue will likely be whether a contract has been formed:

Did A and B form a contract for the sale of B's home to A?

To form a contract at common law, there must be an offer, the offer must be accepted, and the agreement must be supported by consideration.

But you cannot just apply this rule quite yet. You need to lay out whether there is an offer. Your answer should continue like this:

The question now becomes whether B made an offer to A.

An offer must be promissory in character, create a reasonable belief in the offeree that acceptance will conclude the bargain, and state a price for the promise.

Here, there is likely not an offer. B said he would love for someone to take it off his hands. This is not promissory language that seems binding. B did not say I will sell or shall sell or promise to sell. Rather, B merely expressed his desire for someone to take it off B's hands it at some unspecific price and some unspecified time in the future. A reasonable person would not think that merely saying "I accept" would complete a bargain. B's language is indefinite in nature and uses the subjunctive suggesting a statement contrary to fact, he "would love" someone to take it off his hands, not that he is presently seeking someone to purchase the house. Moreover, a real estate transaction is often much more complicated than a couple of exchanged oral statements at the mailbox. Most people would think there are a number of documents and inspections and other processes involved before you can purchase a home making it less likely A could reasonably believe that merely saying "accept" would mean A and B have an enforceable deal for the sale of the house.

Although it is objective manifestations rather than any secret intent that prevails, the fact that A and B laughed at the end of their conversation helps demonstrate that reasonable people would not likely think of anything in this exchange creating an enforceable deal. B also did not state any price term. Although under the UCC the lack of a price term is not fatal to the existence of an offer, this contract is governed by the common law, where price terms are generally considered essential.

Accordingly, the lack of a price term and the nature of the language make it unlikely that this set of statements is an offer that can be merely accepted to create a contract.

You should then move on to whether any possible offer has been accepted and whether there is any consideration to support this possible contract.

Let's do the same with our torts rules. Here is a really brief hypothetical that implicates the rules we have on our index cards for torts:

A, B, and C were all passengers on a subway. A and B were seated across from each other, tossing a baseball back and forth for several minutes during the train ride without event. C was seated two seats away from B with C's briefcase in the seat between B and C. A tossed the ball to B, who tossed it back. A tossed the ball back toward B, but B did not catch the ball, which struck C's briefcase sitting on the seat next to C, knocking the briefcase to the floor.

Has A committed a battery on C?

* * *

The issue is whether A has battered C by touching C's briefcase.

A battery occurs when the actor acts intentionally, causing a touching of the victim, that is harmful or offensive to a reasonable person. To act intentionally means to engage in conduct that is intentional even though the actor does not intend the consequences her actions. An actor acts intentionally where she engages in conduct that is substantially certain to cause a touching. A touching includes physical contact with the victim's person, including items intimately associated with the victim.

Here, A is probably not liable for battery. A has likely acted intentionally. The fact that A and B were playing catch on the subway for several minutes without any indication that anyone else was touched by the ball suggests that A intended to throw the ball to B, not at C or anyone else. However, a subway car is a relatively small and enclosed space and subway seats are usually very close together. It is easy to conceive that throwing a ball at an intended target, particularly to a person, can result in the ball going slightly off target or the target person missing the ball, resulting in a touching of the person seated in the next and very closely situated seat. Thus, it may be substantially certain that a throw in a subway may veer and strike a different target, even if that result is not subjectively intended. A court could conclude that A's act is intentional.

A, however, has not committed an actionable touching, even if his conduct was intentional. The ball did not touch C's person – his physical body. The ball also did not touch any of C's clothes or anything he was carrying. The ball touched C's briefcase, which was not itself connected to C in any way at the time of the contact as it was sitting in the seat next to C. Being hit by a baseball would likely be harmful or offensive to a reasonable person because baseballs are hard objects that, especially when thrown with any velocity to speak of, can cause serious physical injury as evidenced by the fact that baseball players routinely wear helmets while at bat and catchers and umpires wear very thick and comprehensive safety gear to protect themselves from thrown baseballs. However, A is likely not liable for battery because there is no cognizable touching here.

Accordingly, A is likely not liable for battering C because A may not have acted intentionally but more likely because A touched C's briefcase sitting on an adjacent seat and did not touch C's person or an item connected to C.

Let's conclude with a short hypothetical from civil procedure.

Student was born and raised in State A. When Student was 16 years old, she had surgery in State A and the Doctor, a citizen of State A, botched the surgery, causing Student serious physical harm and the loss of a limb. When Student turned 18 years old, she moved to State B to attend college. After moving to State B, Student sued Doctor in federal court in State A claiming that Doctor negligently operated on Student and seeking $100,000 in damages. Doctor moved to dismiss Student's claims against Doctor for lack of subject matter jurisdiction. At a deposition, Student testified that she moved to State B to attend architectural school and intends to finish degree in 4 years. Student testified that she might return to State A but is not sure whether she will do so. Student also said her goal is get a job as an architect and that she would go wherever she found work, including staying in State B if a job presented itself.

How should the court rule on Doctor's motion to dismiss?

* * *

The issue before the court is whether the court should grant or deny the Doctor's motion to dismiss, which turns on whether the federal court has subject matter jurisdiction over Student's lawsuit.

A federal court has diversity of citizenship subject matter jurisdiction to hear state law claims between parties who are citizens of different states and where the amount in controversy exceeds the sum or value of $75,000, exclusive of interest and costs. A natural person who is a U.S. citizen is a citizen of the state in which she is domiciled, meaning the state in which she physically resides with the intent to remain indefinitely. A person intends to remain indefinitely when she has no fixed plan to leave. A natural person may also change her domicile by moving to a new state with the intent to remain in that state indefinitely. A person does not lose her old domicile unless and until a new domicile is established and may only have one state domicile at a time. A court will accept a plaintiff's good faith pleading of damages as satisfying the amount in controversy unless it appears beyond doubt that the plaintiff could never recover more than the minimum amount in controversy.

Here, the facts state that the defendant Doctor is a citizen of State A. The facts also state that the plaintiff Student is suing in federal court for $100,000, which is more than the minimum amount in controversy of $75,000. $100,000 also seems like a feasible demand for damages for a loss of a limb. The question turns on whether Student is domiciled in State A or State B. First, Student appears to be a U.S. citizen having been born in a state of the United States, State A. At least until she was 18, Student appears to have been domiciled in State A because she was born and raised in State A and lived nowhere else until she moved to State B for college. It appears Student likely changed her domicile and thus her citizenship to State B. She currently physically resides in State B because she is attending college there.

She also likely intends to remain there indefinitely. She testified that she is there for college, particularly architectural school, and intends to stay for at least 4 years. Although this suggests she may be transitory like many college students may be, she also testified that she does not have a firm plan to leave. She might move back to State A; she might not. She also testified that getting a job is her goal and that her plan may result in her moving anywhere. However, she has no definite plan to move to any particular state and acknowledges that her plans include potentially staying in State B after graduating. As a result, she plans to stay in State B indefinitely. With Student domiciled in and thus a citizen of State B and Doctor a citizen of State A, the parties are citizens of separate states. Because the parties are diverse and the amount in controversy is met, the court has diversity of citizenship subject matter jurisdiction.

Accordingly, Student is likely a citizen of State B and Doctor is a citizen of State A making the parties diverse and vesting the federal court with subject matter jurisdiction based on diversity of citizenship; thus, the court should deny the defendant Doctor's motion to dismiss based on lack of subject matter jurisdiction.

Note that I have tried to use visual separation to make it clear my answer consists of four parts: an issue statement or initial conclusion (I or C), a rule section (R), an analysis or application section (A), and an ultimate conclusion (C). This is the standard format – often abbreviated as IRAC or CRAC – that your professor is looking for in response to legal essay questions.

If your professor has past exams you can look at, by all means review them. If your professor also gives out model or sample answers, you should also review those BUT do not read the answers until you have attempted to write your own answer! Find out how long the professor gave students to answer the essay hypothetical. Set a timer. Then write or type out your answer and be brutal about stopping when time is up. Then you should compare your answer to the model or sample answer the professor provided. Do this with as many past essay hypotheticals as you can find.

5

Conclusion

The time you spend memorizing these rules will allow you to quickly recite the ones you need and to do so with a high degree of accuracy. That frees you up to think. Rather than having to use your preciously limited time and energy during the exam to think about what the rules are, you can think about how the facts in the hypothetical satisfy or do not satisfy the words of the rules you know by heart.

My hope is that following this method gives you a workable plan of attack for your exams. I hope that breeds confidence, reduces anxiety, and results in excellent essay exam answers!

If you like this book or have had success with it, please take a moment to leave a review.

Good luck!

About the Author

Associate Professor Eric Porterfield joined the inaugural faculty of UNT Dallas College of Law in June 2014, after serving as a Visiting Assistant Professor of Law at Texas Tech University School of Law, where he taught Legal Writing and advanced classes in the areas of Civil Procedure and Evidence. Professor Porterfield teaches Civil Procedure, Evidence, and upper division procedural courses. He was granted tenure in Fall 2019.

In 2017, Professor Porterfield co-authored and published *Civil Procedure in Focus* (with Professor Jeremy Counseller), a Federal Civil Procedure casebook that provides students accessible explanatory text and opportunities to apply the law to multiple sets of facts in every chapter.

In 2001, Professor Porterfield earned his B.A. from the University of Texas at Austin with highest honors with a double major of Government and German, and was inducted into Phi Beta Kappa and the National

Golden Key Honor Society. In 2004, Professor Porterfield graduated as the Valedictorian of his law school class at Baylor Law School, earning his J.D. degree summa cum laude. He earned the highest score in the class in many of his first year classes, including Contracts, Civil Procedure, Criminal Law, and Torts. He also served as Senior Executive Editor of the Baylor Law Review, making initial publication decisions, and as Managing Editor of the 2004 edition of Texas Practice, Baylor's inaugural special issue focusing on Texas evidence and procedure.

Also while at Baylor, Professor Porterfield competed successfully in several advocacy competitions. His team won the inaugural 2003 National Association of Criminal Defense Lawyers Mock Trial Tournament and he was named the Best Oral Advocate of the competition as his team went undefeated to claim the championship. His team also claimed the Regional Championship of the 2004 Association of Trial Lawyers of America (now AAJ) Mock Trial Competition, beating another Baylor team in the finals, and was a National semi-finalist, placing third on points overall. His brief was also named Third Best Brief of the 2002 New York Bar Association Moot Court Tournament.

After graduating from Baylor, Professor Porterfield served as a law clerk to the Honorable David C. Godbey, United States District Judge for the Northern District of Texas, Dallas Division. While a law clerk to Judge Godbey, Professor Porterfield was an assistant coach of Baylor's National Championship Mock Trial Team in the 2005 ATLA Competition. The Texas House of Representatives issued a congratulatory Resolution describing the school's success in the 2003, 2004, and 2005 competitions. See Texas House Resolution 2058 (May 26, 2005).

Professor Porterfield then joined Carrington Coleman, a large Dallas law firm. He defended a variety of medical and legal professionals in malpractice and administrative licensure actions, health care institutions in a variety of matters, and corporations in multi-national disputes, helping to resolve a global dispute in London involving parties from three continents. While at Carrington Coleman, he was active in pro bono work for the Dallas Volunteer Attorney Program, helping victims of domestic violence and exploited consumers. He also served on the Board of Directors of the Dallas Wind Symphony from 2006-2009.

In 2009, Professor Porterfield joined Lee Brown at the Brown Law Firm in Dallas – a firm specializing in complex automotive product defect cases. He represented catastrophically injured consumers in these complex cases against car manufacturers and automotive component suppliers from around the world. Professor Porterfield has tried several multi-week product liability cases and has litigated these cases in federal and state courts across the country, from Hawaii to New York, at all stages, from pretrial through trial and appeals, including briefing to intermediate courts of appeals and the Texas Supreme Court.

In 2012, Professor Porterfield left the Brown Law Firm to pursue an LL.M. degree from Harvard Law School. While at Harvard, he researched and specialized in international civil litigation and published his first article with the Temple Law Review, entitled "Too Much Process, Not Enough Service: International Service of Process Under the Hague Service Convention," a critique of the treaty governing international service of process, including suggestions for reform. He graduated from Harvard Law School in 2013 and his LL.M. Thesis, which earned Honors marks, focuses on reforming personal jurisdiction and judgment enforcement rules, including a critique of the Hague Judgments Convention. A revised and expanded version of this thesis was published in the Duke Journal of Comparative and International Law, entitled "A Domestic Proposal to Revive the Hague Judgments Convention: How to Stop Worrying about Streams, Trickles, Asymmetry, and a Lack of Reciprocity" in 2015. He is a frequent author and presenter on continuing education materials from legal writing to procedural rules and continues to research and write in the areas of Civil Procedure and Evidence.

You can connect with me on:

https://www.untdallas.edu/lawschool

Also by Eric Porterfield

Civil Procedure in Focus

https://www.aspenpublishing.com/counseller-civprofocus2

Civil Procedure in Focus by Jeremy Counseller and Eric Porterfield uses a combination of accessible explanatory text, cases, and other primary legal sources to teach civil procedure, and then provides opportunities for students to apply the law to multiple sets of facts in every chapter. Selected cases illustrate key changes in the law and show how courts have developed and apply doctrine.

The unintimidating approach of this casebook provides a hands-on, experiential learning environment that can be essential to many students' success. Through practice-based exercises, students learn to apply legal principles and concepts to real-world scenarios. Simply knowing the facts of a benchmark case is not enough; knowing how to apply the doctrine from one case to a *different* set of facts enhances a student's ability to succeed in and after law school.

Made in the USA
Monee, IL
04 November 2026

67386625R00036